BERLIN

CAPE TOWN

PALMA DE MALLORCA

REYKJAVÍK

MILAN

TBILISI

COPYRIGHT

The publisher would like to thank the following for their kind permission to reproduce their photographs:

Erin Wulfsohn (@erinwulfsohn) for Pursch Artistes (@purschartistes) p.7, picture on the bottom; Robin Benzrihem p. 10; Hotel Hoxton p.14-17; Hôtel Henriette, Hervé Goluza, p.18, 21; Hôtel Henriette, p.20; Hotel Monte Cristo, Christophe Bielsa p.22-25; Hôtel National Des Arts et Métiers, Jérôme Galland p.26-29; Hotel Brach, Yann Audic p.34; Hotel Brach, Volodin p.36; Hotel Brach, Guillaumede de Laubier p.37; Hotel Panache, Romain Ricard p.38-41; Hotel Nolinski, Guillaume de Laubier p.41-45; Hôtel des Grands Boulevards p.46-49; Le Roch Hotel & Spa p.50-53; Archive 18-20 p.188; The Broken Arm, François Coquerel p.198; MOB Hotel, Aldo Paredes p.216; MOB Hotel, Cyrille Weiner p.218.

PARIS

CITY GUIDE *for* DESIGN LOVERS

The Travel Colours City Guides are for design-loving travellers who like to explore the trendiest places in each city, for travellers who see themselves as trendsetters. Each City Guide features a curated selection of the best places to "sleep, eat, drink, shop and explore", all of which have been personally tried and tested.

Edition ONE

EDITOR IN CHIEF
STEFANIE FRIESE

PHOTOGRAPHY BY
FLAVIA RENZ

WORDS BY
HANNI HEINRICH

TRENDSCOUT
NIKKI WANG, FREDERIC BOURGEOIS

PUBLISHED BY
FRIESE MEDIA GMBH, 2019
1ST EDITION - SEPTEMBER 2019

PRINTED AND BOUND BY
HARTMANNDRUCK & MEDIEN GMBH IN GERMANY ON FSC CERTIFIED UNCOATED PAPER

ISBN 978-3-9821148-0-4

SAY HELLO

GENERAL ENQUIRIES: hello@travelcolours.de
DISTRIBUTION: sales@travelcolours.de

GET THE BOOKS ONLINE AT

www.travelcolours.guide

WE TAKE CARE

OF YOU AND OF MOTHER EARTH

We work closely with a family-run printing company that has been printing climate-neutral for years together with ClimatePartner. All our books are printed exclusively on FSC-certified paper.

NIKKI WANG

TREND SCOUT, PARIS

The French art de vivre is what inspired Beijing-born Nikki to come to Paris. Together with Frederic, they founded TheWaysBeyond, a concept store of cultural activities: *www.thewaysbeyond.fr*

FREDERIC BOURGEOIS

TREND SCOUT, PARIS

Frederic worked for several cultural institutions before he moved to Paris and met Nikki. Together, they share an endless curiosity for culture, good food and all the important things in life.

STEFANIE FRIESE

FOUNDER & EDITOR IN CHIEF

It has to be nice and a bit different. The desire for lifestyle and design is always guaranteed. As the founder of Travel Colours, Stefanie is always in search of the most beautiful places.

FLAVIA RENZ

PHOTOGRAPHER

Being based in Berlin, Flavia loves to keep herself surrounded by all that is beautiful and yummy. You usually find her standing on any furniture available, just to get that picture framed perfectly.

HANNI HEINRICH

EDITOR

As a writer, Hanni is inspired by people, human behaviour and beaches. Her favourite body lotion is sun blocker factor 50. Born in Merseburg, Germany, she is currently based in Cape Town.

LOVE LETTER

Poets, artists, and writers have all written about their love of Paris. It's hard not to fall in love with this city – a place of elegance, sophistication and style. Paris is the home of haute couture and exquisite cuisine. In fact, the art of French cooking owes its success to the mastery of classic basics updated by today's chefs. It's known that the French prefer quality to quantity, especially when it comes to food.

And the glimmering Seine with its elegant bridges has arguably made Paris the most recognisable and romanticised cityscape in the world.

Paris holds hundreds of years of history – of monarchy, revolution, revolt and artistic innovation – and at the same time, Paris radiates with increasingly futuristic architecture and lifestyle concepts. In 2024 Paris will show a new vision of Olympism in action, celebrating its unique spirit of old and new, and everything in between.

Spending long afternoons getting lost in the Louvre or exploring the Musée d'Orsay are possible as well as discovering plenty of contemporary life in the less tourist-trodden outer arrondissements.

Stefanie Friese

EDITOR IN CHIEF

SLEEP

THE HOXTON, PARIS

HOUSED IN A HÔTEL PARTICULIER

This hotel is well placed for visiting Paris' more traditional attractions, with the Louvre and the Seine just 20 minutes away on foot. Located in the 2nd arrondissement, The Hoxton guarantees Instagram satisfaction with period details of the original 18th-century hôtel particulier blending with on-point décor from the Soho House creatives.

The building was once the residence of Etienne Rivié, adviser to Louis XV, adding original French flair. All 172 rooms are fitted out to the same specification with categories based purely on size: Shoebox; Cosy; Roomy; Biggy. The atmosphere is relaxed and comfortable, and the multilingual staff from all over the world create a lively international vibe.

30-32 Rue du Sentier, 75002 Paris
www.thehoxton.com/paris/paris/hotels

HÔTEL HENRIETTE

BOHEMIAN DESIGN HOTEL

This pretty boutique hotel makes a cosy and romantic base for a city break in Paris. Hotel Henriette is located on a relatively quiet side street, five minutes' walk from the vibrant Rue Mouffetard and the historic Latin Quarter. The Luxembourg Gardens, as well as the Jardin des Plantes botanical gardens and zoo, are also within walking distance. Hotel Henriette is an Instagrammer's dream. Fashion journalist and designer Vanessa Scoffier has colour-blocked walls and combined fresh wooden floors with splashes of floral patterns to give the hotel its bohemian chic touch. Each of the 32 rooms is a little different and the tasty buffet breakfast is served in a bright room overlooking the winter garden.

9 Rue des Gobelins, 75013 Paris
www.hotelhenriette.com

HOTEL MONTE CRISTO

19TH-CENTURY CHARM WITH MODERN-DAY COMFORTS

Tucked away on a side street in the 5th arrondissement, Hotel Monte Cristo offers 19th-century charm coupled with modern-day comforts. Fifty rooms and a 16-metre swimming pool are available for guests' comfort and enjoyment. Rumour has it that long ago Paris' first rum bar was here. That's why Monte Cristo provides a selection of the best rums, vintages, flavoured rums and special rums for the initiated and connoisseurs, and a flavoursome journey accompanied by a cellar master and head bartender. The hotel's high standards can be measured in the sophisticated details. Over 200 period pieces lend the hotel an inimitable patina. Trophies of stuffed animals, like a curiosity cabinet, greet guests when entering the hotel.

20-22 Rue Pascal, 75005 Paris
www.hotelmontecristoparis.com

HÔTEL NATIONAL DES ARTS ET MÉTIERS

FACTORY-CHIC INTERIORS

Located on the border between the neighbourhoods of Montorgueil and Le Haut Marais, the Hôtel National des Arts et Métiers complements the building's historic character with innovative design and exceptional craftsmanship. It has even floors that house some 66 rooms of various types – most have balconies or terraces. All the rooms have designer cuddle chairs and the finest Parisian linens. If the budget permits, the Penthouse is the one to book. A variety of places to eat and drink can be found on the ground floor and on the rooftop. The hotel is also committed to sustainable development and has conceptualised an ecological policy covering the products and consumables provided for guests.

243 Rue Saint-Martin, 75003 Paris
www.hotelnational.paris

HÔTEL ALFRED SOMMIER

A FORMER FAMILY MANSION

The hôtel particulier of sugar industrialist Alfred Sommier has been restored by a family descendant as a luxury hotel. The soul of the family mansion has been preserved. A series of spacious and bright reception rooms strikes once upon entering the hotel. A checkerboard white and garnet-red marble floor accentuates the perspective and two majestic marble staircases stand at each extremity. Family souvenirs arouse curiosity. A private garden offering either sun or shade is hidden in the heart of the mansion. It is rare to find luxurious Parisian hotels that have such a unique garden where one can enjoy a meal, a drink, or just relax while admiring the cut stone façades.

20 Rue de l'Arcade, 75008 Paris
www.alfredsommier.com

HOTEL BRACH

DESIGNED BY PHILIPPE STARCK

This hotel in the 16th arrondissement offers a modern take on luxury combined with a strong design slant. It is not the most vibrant part of town, but still has plenty of Parisian charm. The hotel sits atop a vast subterranean sports space – complete with 22-metre pool – loosely modelled on a 1930s boxing gym with the use of unfinished concrete and a few judiciously placed vintage running machines. All rooms are generously proportioned. Designs vary and spaces are dominated by rich wood panelling, plush patterned carpets and finished with homely touches such as framed sketches leaned against the wall. A curated selection of French novels and art books complete the Parisian charm.

1-7 Rue Jean Richepin, 75016 Paris
www.brachparis.com

HOTEL PANACHE

FOR A TRENDY STAY

Situated at the corner of Rue du Faubourg Montmartre and Rue Geoffroy Marie, Hotel Panache provides a home for all who love throbbing day and nightlife in Paris. Panache embraces Art Nouveau: the hotel was inspired by the Flatiron Building in New York. The interior reflects geometric rhythms on the walls.

The hotel supports the community and whenever a craftsman is needed it uses the services of a local. The breakfast and dessert menus are designed by NOGLU – the first gluten-free restaurant to open in Paris. Each room's mini-bar is also stocked with chocolates from La Mere de Famille, the oldest chocolate factory in Paris.

1 Rue Geoffroy-Marie, 75009 Paris
www.hotelpanache.com

HOTEL NOLINSKI

CONTEMPORARY LUXURY HOTEL

The Nolinski is located in the heart of Paris, near the Palais-Royal, close to the Louvre Museum and the Opéra Garnier. It is an ode to beauty by day and the City of Lights by night. This hotel celebrates Paris: from the romance of the Seine to the formidable majesty of the Palais Royal's sun-drenched gardens, the Nolinski has it all. The rooms are bright and luminous and a mineral spa invites guests to let their senses roam and emotions rise. Here unimaginable dreams can come true and every art piece paves the way for every footstep. At the Nolinski, guests wander through a world in which luxurious comforts, art and Parisian lifestyle coexist.

16 Avenue de l'Opéra, 75001 Paris
www.nolinskiparis.com

HÔTEL DES GRANDS BOULEVARDS

18TH-CENTURY PARISIAN ELEGANCE

This 230-year-old building has been transformed into the Hôtel des Grands Boulevards, an ode to 18th-century Paris (think Louis XVI, French Revolution). Situated on the Boulevard Poissonniere in the 2nd arrondissement, the hotel serves as the historical demarcation between the centre's bourgeois neighbourhoods and their popular suburbs. Fifty rooms and a hidden courtyard invite guests to breathe the Parisian air, enjoy A-lister cocktail culture, Franco-Italian cuisine and a magical rooftop. The interior is celebrity French designer Dorothée Meilichzon's signature. Deep colours and clever use of mirrors and designer furniture shine through every gap. This is the third hotel of the successful Experimental Cocktail Group after the Grand Pigalle and Covent Garden's Henrietta Hotel.

17 Boulevard Poissonnière, 75002 Paris
www.grandsboulevardshotel.com

LE ROCH HOTEL & SPA

RELAXING ATMOSPHERE

With its unbeatable location, nestled between the Place Vendôme, the Palais Garnier and the Louvre, the elegant Hotel Le Roch stands out. Tasteful design, with clean lines, attention to detail, soft lighting, and a warm, balanced pastel palette of sage, chartreuse, and milky-green ensure a relaxing and enchanting atmosphere when entering the lobby. Plush, expansive sofas invite one to relax while the lounge and library area invites guests to read by the fireplace. On warm days, the garden in the courtyard invites one to linger. Healthy relaxation awaits at the spa and the private pool as well as at the hammam.

28 Rue Saint-Roch, 75001 Paris
www.leroch-hotel.com

EAT

WITH COFFEE

GRAMME
cuisine parisienne
TAKE-AWAY COFFEE
BREAKFAST
LUNCH
WINE
HOMEMADE

GRAMME

ONLY FRESH SEASONAL INGREDIENTS

This small Parisian canteen café with its beautiful sleek house façade is run by Marine and Romain. While Romain attends to the queuing guests, Marine works magic in the small open kitchen. Most of the guests are returning customers who cannot get enough of the signature dishes, such as brioche perdue – a slice of deep-fried brioche topped with a cream of popcorn and salted butter caramel – or the ever-popular œufs mouillettes. Only quality products and fresh seasonal ingredients are used in the dishes and the owners work in close co-operation with suppliers, who share the same values.

86 Rue des Archives, 75003 Paris

SEASON PARIS

FOR ALL HEALTHY PARISIANS

Ever dreamt of a ménage à trois? Welcome to Season! This restaurant, coffee shop and juice bar offers fresh produce at three locations. The menu changes every season and reflects North American influences. Everything a healthy girl as well as a hungry Parisienne craves can be found at Season. Gluten-free gourmet dishes with plenty of fruit can be enjoyed all day. The breakfast menu is also served all day. Sandwiches and natural cold-pressed juices can be found at Season's three locations: Season Restaurant, Season Take Away and Season Fit. Every Season is bright and colourfully decorated, perfect for immortalisation on Instagram.

1 Rue Charles-François Dupuis, 75003 Paris
www.season-paris.com

CAFE INEKO

MEDITERRANEAN ATMOSPHERE

Located in the Rue des Gravilliers, Cafe Ineko is a warm place, bathed in light that comes directly from the ceiling. Wooden furniture and Beatles' music makes this cafe extra delightful. All bread and pastries are made with carefully selected ingredients, the more natural the better. The desserts are divine (rice with a milk-lemon-coconut floating island with dried fruits) and the service is efficient and calm. What strikes one the most is the benevolence and quality – a kind of fair elegance, so rare in Paris. Ineko is a good place for breakfast and lunch within a solid and sober Mediterranean atmosphere. Famous interior designer François Champsaur, designed the café.

13 Rue des Gravilliers, 75003 Paris

café
MERICOURT
It's Brunch time!
If we are full please
form a line outside we
will come out to give you
a seat

CAFÉ MÉRICOURT

SIMPLE AND DELICIOUS CUISINE

Café Méricourt, at 22 Rue de la Folie Méricourt is the second establishment of Café Oberkampf. The Méricourt serves cuisine that is both simple and delicious, accompanied by specialty coffee. Brunch-lovers will find heaven here from 9am to 3pm in a bright and pastel-coloured atmosphere. The menu offers an assortment of homemade muesli, basil, ricotta and seasonal fruit pancakes, a breakfast bun consisting of an egg, bacon, arugula and chilli jam, not forgetting the famous Shakshuka. The kitchen also offers other specialties, such as a seven-hour lamb leg sandwich, a quinoa "Green Bowl" with avocado, young shoots, pickled vegetables and tahini seasoning. On weekdays, a more traditional dish of the day is offered at lunchtime.

22 Rue de la Folie Méricourt, 75011 Paris
www.cafemericourt.com

If we
form a
will
a seat
Si nous
merci de
qu'on aura

OFFICINE UNIVERSELLE
GRAND CAFÉ TORTONI
CAFETIER • LIMONADIER • GLACIER
fondé à Paris rue Taitbout en 1798
HORAIRES OUVERTURE
DU MARDI AU DIMANCHE
DE 11 heures À 19 heures

GRAND CAFÉ TORTONI

CHIC AND SOCIALITE PARISIAN CAFÉ

An institution on the merry boulevards around the Chaussée d'Antin, the highlight of Parisian pleasures in the 19th century, the Grand Café Tortoni used to attract artists, writers, socialites and comedians and bears the name of its owners, the Italians who introduced ice-cream to France. The Comptoir Tortoni on Rue de Saintonge is mainly appreciated by regulars, a few connoisseurs and fashionistas, but remains one of Paris' best-kept secrets. It offers hot chocolate, lemonade or a quick coffee with a chouquette and home-made pastries.

Opposite, the counter of Officine Universelle Buly displays beauty products and accessories and perfumes. Beneath a glass roof at 45 Rue de Saintonge, Le Comptoir des Services offers exclusive gift-wrapping and personalised services, with a massage room still to come.

45 Rue de Saintonge, 75003 Paris

ABRICOT
Officine Universelle Buly fondée en 1803
LAVANDE
Officine Universelle Buly fondée en 1803

BACK IN BLACK

COLD AND HOT BREWS

Back in Black adds another jewel to Paris' reputation as an exquisite coffee city. Newly opened by KB Coffee roasters, this coffee place is known for brewed drinks, sandwiches, and homemade cakes and scones. It's one of the few cafés with great coffee where it's socially acceptable to pull out a laptop and work. At Back in Black, space is the concept. Lots of space. While baristas prepare cold and hot brews in front of the coffee machines, visitors can enjoy a cup in quietness, read a newspaper, or enjoy homemade buns, bread or granola for breakfast. The lunch options are, of course also delicious at this coffee roasting. The interior is, of course, black, modern and industrial.

25 Rue Amelot, 75011 Paris
www.backinblackcoffee.com

KB
KB

NEIGHBOURS

AUSTRALIAN STYLE COFFEE SHOP

Neighbours is the second location from the Australian couple who founded the critically acclaimed Honor. Neighbours is a friendly, welcoming hub for locals, friends and travellers. Cosy in size, it is like an extension of one's kitchen and living room. The focus is on great coffee and fresh tasty food with Australian/British roots for breakfast, lunch and brunch. The specialty is their sourdough crumpets. Soft yet crispy they are perfect for scrambled eggs or smashed avocado. It fills up quickly, especially on weekends when Parisian brunchers descend in droves, but there's also outdoor seating on the sun filled terrace. Rumour has it that Neighbours makes the best coffee in town so make sure to put it on your coffee crawl list.

89 Boulevard Beaumarchais, 75003 Paris
www.neighbours.paris

MAISON
ALIMENTATION

MAISON PLISSON SAINT-HONORÉ

DEVOTED TO LOCAL PRODUCTS

This establishment has revolutionised Paris' gastronomic landscape. Maison Plisson is the first concept entirely dedicated to common sense and pleasure in food. Located in a 1900 building in the Marais district and Place du Marché Saint-Honoré just near by Place Vendôme, Maison Plisson is devoted to exclusively local products. There is a grocery store with 5 000 different delicacies, a bakery, a cellar with 500 wines, and a covered market. Whether for take away or sit down, or even catering an event, Maison Plisson satisfies every wish.

A restaurant with a terrace seduces the taste buds and invites visitors to unwind. And the long opening hours of this exceptional department store are perfectly adapted to the rhythm of the city.

35 Place du Marché Saint-Honoré, 75001 Paris
www.lamaisonplisson.com

LES RÉSISTANTS

LOCAL INGREDIENTS FOR GOURMANDS

Who is the "resistance"? Les Résistants is a fine-dining restaurant; the fulfilled dream of childhood friends who are passionate about cooking and good food. Their idea: creating a restaurant that would be a direct link between local producers and gourmands. Priority is given to the discovery of products, wines, tastes, producers, winemakers and all olfactory sensations. Transparency is obvious because every taste bud and everybody knows what comes in and where it came from. This restaurant's motto is "To feed well while respecting the natural cycles". All dishes on the daily-changing small menu are made from ingredients from local producers and the wine list offers natural wines.

16-18 Rue du Château d'Eau, 75010 Paris
www.lesresistants.fr

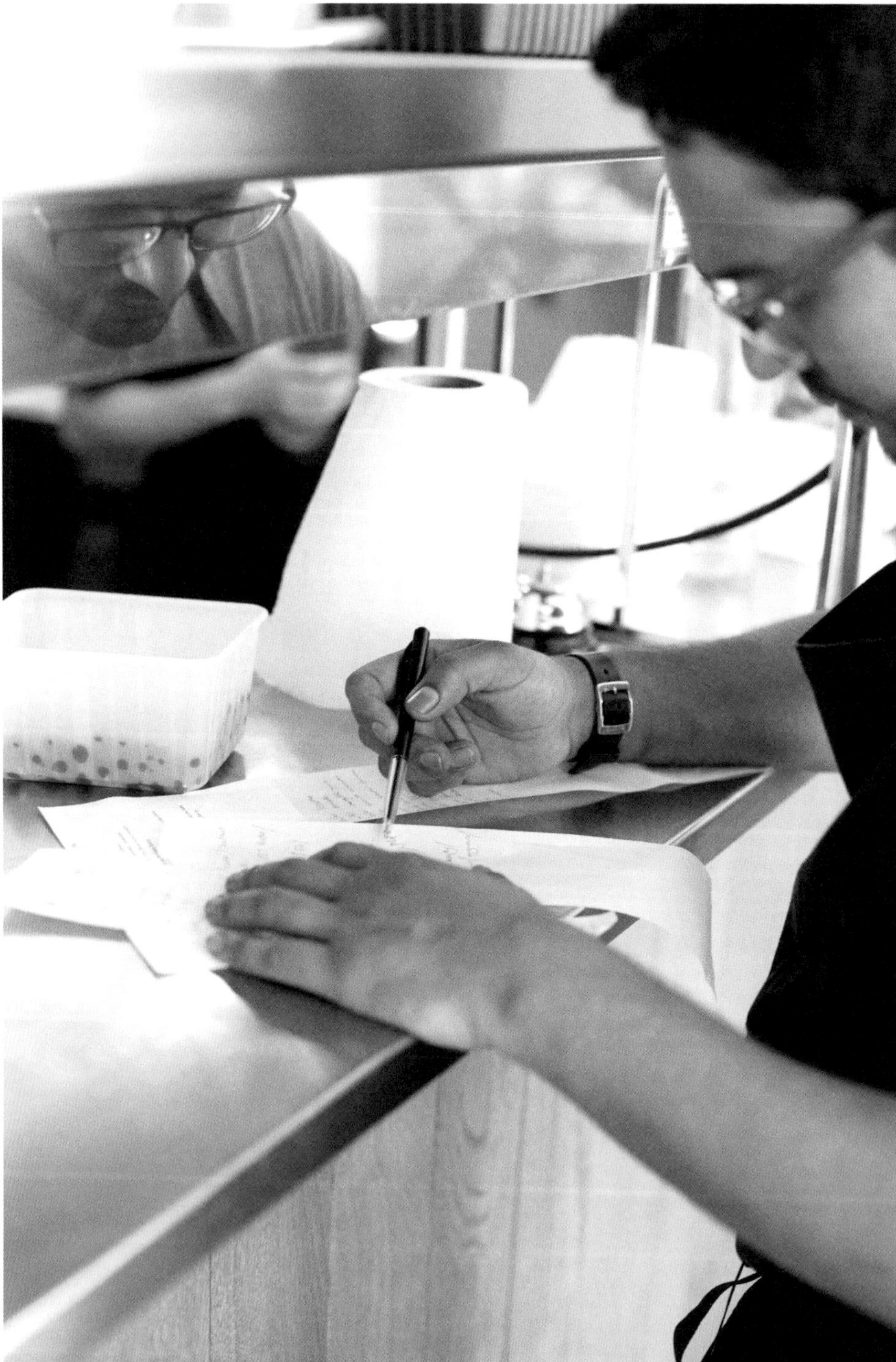

CRAVAN

COCKTAIL BAR-CAFÉ

Cravan offers two in one: coffee and cocktails. This bar is a paradise for all coffee and experimental drink lovers. Cravan even invented a cult drink called The Tunnel – a revisited negroni – to start the evening. The counter and old antique wooden chairs are inviting when one passes the door of this Art Nouveau-classified historical monument. Cravan is extreme: no wine, no beer. Only cocktails and coffee. Open every day from 8am to get the day started while reading a newspaper, or to simply share a plate of white Landes asparagus – the star food of the moment. Also for night owls, the Cravan proposes a few liquid tasters from the book French Modern Cocktails from the 1920s &1930s. On weekends, this bar offers a Sunday roast to relax over and get ready for the new week.

17 Rue Jean de la Fontaine, 75016 Paris

EAT

WITH WINE

CANTINA

FINE MEAT, GOOD WINE

At Cantina everything is grilled at the parilla the famous Argentinian barbecue. Located in the 10th arrondissement next to the Canal Saint-Martin, this little cantina already stands as the new Messi. Sabrina Goldin and Stephane Abby have created a bastion that transports one directly to South America. Fine meat, good wine and the long communal table invite everyone to relax and enjoy. The typical penguin carafe adds Argentinian zest. The cantina burger, a juicy steak, smoked scamorza, aioli and tangy ketchup sends one directly to heaven. A beautiful dish, a flan of sweet milk (dulce de leche) with amber and caramelised notes, is well worth tasting.

11 Rue Marie et Louise, 75010 Paris
www.theasadoclub.com

FRENCHIE
bar à vins

FRENCHIE

ONE-STAR MICHELIN RESTAURANT

Star Chef Greg Marchand opened Frenchie to create a place he would want to go back to again and again. The products change with the seasons and the dishes are based on French fundamentals, inspired by an international repertoire. For lunch, patrons can choose between a three-course menu and the chef's carte blanche menu. At dinner, the chef expresses his culinary creativity in a five-course tasting menu. Frenchie is a one-star Michelin restaurant newly awarded in 2019. The concept has since been expanded to FTG, which serves classic American and British street food with a French twist. Greg has revitalised the once sleepy Rue du Nil into a mile of flavour and delicacies.

5 Rue du Nil, 75002 Paris
www.frenchie-ruedunil.com

FRENCHIE
Greg Marchand

MAISON MAISON

DRINKS AND FOOD WITH A VIEW

Have a Paris food affair. Maison Maison is a restaurant and mini wine bar, located on the banks of the Seine facing Pont Neuf to the left with the classic Parisian buildings behind. And to the right, the always beautiful Eiffel Tower in the distance. Indulge in Saucisson, ham, burrata, sauteed shishito peppers, or lentil soup, cockles with diced buttered broth, and a sweet pear tart. The atmosphere is romantic, joyful and full of life. Maison Maison is a place for laughter and summer excitement because everyone's happy to be in Paris, drinking wine and staring at some of the most beautiful views a city can offer.

Face au, 16 Quai du Louvre, 75001 Paris

PATISSERIE
LIGNAC

EELS

CONTEMPORARY KITCHEN

Young chef Adrien Ferrand knows how to flirt – with food. This restaurant brings out the eel in an outstanding way and uses seasonal products for all dishes. The cuisine is energetic and contrasted with cosmopolitan influences from Asia, Spain and Italy. So then, what's on the menu? For example, fillet of trout served characteristically, but not overly, pink, with green asparagus and a bouillabaisse sauce and a much richer, deboned, grilled quail stuffed with foie gras, lightened by fresh peas and baby broad beans – all with beautifully judged seasonings and textures. The atmosphere is young, which makes fine dining a fun experience here. The carefully selected wine menu comes directly from the producer.

27 Rue d'Hauteville, 75010 Paris
www.restaurant-eels.com

ROBERT

MODERN EUROPEAN CUISINE

From Adelaide to Paris, Robert Restaurant has only one vision: good food, good wine and a welcoming warm ambience. Australian chef Peter Orr and the collaboration from Martin, Loïc Martin and Edouard Bergeon, create a genuine link between the earth and the plate. The farmers work hand in hand with the restaurant and vice versa to source quality products. Robert is located in Paris' 11th arrondissement and serves modern European cuisine, based on seasonal local products, that's why the wines are predominantly from France. As natural as the dishes are, so is the interior. Wooden floors and white walls create a warm atmosphere while flower bouquets emphasise the garden-like feeling. Peter left home when he was only 19 and now, aged 32, he is living his dream and calls Paris home.

32 Rue de la Fontaine au Roi, 75011 Paris
www.robert-restaurant.fr

LA CUISINE LIBANAISE
SALMA HAGE
PHAIDON
MICHAEL CONNELLY LE POÈTE

FULGURANCES

A STAGE FOR YOUNG CHEFS TO PERFORM

This concept is a fine-dining restaurant and a wine bar that acts as an incubator, welcoming young chefs to take over the kitchen to find and refine their identity. Fulgurances is a stage for chefs to perform and train. It is a loving triangle honouring good food, tasty wines and creating events around taste and tasting. Fulgurances is also a consultancy agency for events in the gastronomic industry where aesthetics has always been an important part.

10 Rue Alexandre Dumas, 75011 Paris
www.fulgurances.com

MAMIE PAR JEAN IMBERT

INSPIRED BY HIS GRANDMOTHER

In the 16th arrondissement is a restaurant that makes gourmands hearts beat faster; it's where celebrity and star chef Jean Imbert rules. During the French TV Show "Top Chef", Imbert impressed the jury's taste buds and made friends with JR and Pharell Williams. His restaurant, Mamie Jean Imbert, is run in partnership with his charismatic grandmother, whom he has to thank for his passion for cuisine. Popular dishes on the menu are crêpe Suzette or a juicy stuffed tomato or chicken with mashed potatoes and herbal juice. Almost every ingredient comes from France, that's why there's no octopus or avocado at Mamie. Today, Imbert owns five establishments in Paris and one in Miami.

35bis Rue Jean de la Fontaine, 75016 Paris
www.mamiejeanimbert.com

VERJUS

FULL OF FINESSE

Small, but with a kitchen full of finesse, this is worth a stop. This tiny restaurant serves products of exquisite quality with unmistakable finesse on the plate. Located on Rue de Richelieu, one has to go through an unmarked iron gate, up some well-worn steps and through a plain grey-painted door to enter the restaurant. Then, magic happens: indulge in a tasting menu that mixes a modest amount of meat or fish with some of the best vegetable creations. The restaurant has put together an incredible wine list that is heavy with organic and biodynamic producers. Verjus processes the ingredients like rough diamonds – no wonder this dining room enjoys recognition across Paris. Its flair is both charmingly at ease and elegantly distinctive. Verjus is a genuine thrill.

52 Rue de Richelieu, 75001 Paris
www.verjusparis.com

IBRIK KITCHEN

ROMANIAN CUISINE

Ibrik is situated in the 2nd arrondissement in Rue de Mulhouse and is the personification of delicious rustic Mediterranean cooking. Ibrik combines tradition and modernity. This art-gallery-like little restaurant focuses on meze and appetisers, most meant to be shared. Daily lunch specials lure hungry Parisians inside to have a rustic and healthy meal and relax. But the real experience is at dinner time when steaming dishes are presented in various creative ways. The lucky diners getting a table in the evening will enjoy a sophisticated and relaxed time dipping food into the hummus. The desserts are all made in-house and the recommended pistachio cake packed with bright green nuts is pure happiness.

43 Rue Laffitte, 75009 Paris
www.ibrik.fr

BONHOMIE

MEDITERRANEAN WITH A MODERN TWIST

Bonhomie celebrates the love of enjoyment and is a playground for chefs, bartenders and baristas. The menu at Bonhomie is Mediterranean with a modern twist, with the best and freshest ingredients being delivered daily. It changes regularly according to what is in season and features vegetarian dishes as well as meat and fish. Bonhomie's food is soulful, made for sharing with friends and lovers! Tapas is the favourite and combined with wine will satisfy all the senses of every guest. Bonhomie is the first dining venture from the group behind Parisian cocktail bars Little Red Door and Lulu White, which bring the elements coffee, craft cocktails and Mediterranean small plates together harmoniously.

22 Rue d'Enghien, 75010 Paris
www.bonhomie.paris

MARGÚS

GOOD VIBES ONLY

Margús is a family story with a taste of elsewhere. Immediately upon entering the restaurant, one might get the feeling of being in a slightly faded Cuba. Family photos support the fact that Maria Margarita, nicknamed Margús, is the queen here. She is the inspirational grandmother of the venue's founders, Jean-Charles and Alexandre. This family explores and plays with South American flavours with verve and panache, which leaves a savour of spicy surprise on the lips. Tacos, tapas and sliced meats are in the spotlight, accompanied, of course, by carefully selected beverages. At Margús, it's all about a good atmosphere.

1 Rue des Prouvaires, 75001 Paris
www.margus.fr

LE CHEVAL D'OR

SOPHISTICATED FRENCH-ASIAN RESTAURANT

This French-Asian restaurant is the talk of the town. Chef Taku Sekine is one of Paris' most popular. Only 50 bar buns are made each day made from seasonal fresh products and deep delicious flavours. Of course, the all-natural wines match the high-quality food ingredients. The menu is a mix of small and larger dishes presented according to the cooking, seasoning and the choice of ingredients (hors d'oeuvre, raw, steamed, deep-fried, flour, sides, noodles, rice ...). The presentation is sophisticated: Chinese bamboo basket, traditional French crockery and Japanese containers for green tea. Located in the 19th arrondissement, gourmands will find lots of delicious a la carte choices to share.

8 Rue des Panoyaux, 75020 Paris
www.lechevalenor.fr

PAPILLON

CAREFULLY PREPARED DISHES

This intimate and Nordic-looking restaurant is open Monday to Friday. A 13-metre custom-designed façade metal-embossed in 1965-style with rounded and smooth lines makes Papillon recognisable. Chef and owner Christophe Saintagne took the kitchen out of the basement to flood it with natural light and provide a view. For lunch or dinner, all dishes are carefully prepared with the finest ingredients and presented on Pillivuyt French porcelain, adding a further feel of elegance. Adjacent to the main dining room, are cosy corners for romantic candlelight dinner dates. Blond wood Stia chairs and caramel-coloured leather benches emphasise warm tones.

8 Rue Meissonier, 75017 Paris
www.papillonparis.fr

LE CHARDENOUX

INNOVATIVE CUISINE

For over 100 years this restaurant has kept its authentic values and innovative cuisine. Till today Le Chardenoux is an institution in Paris. Situated on Rue Jules Valles, Le Chardenoux reflects elegance from its decorative foliated ceiling to the listed marble bar front. Designed with charm and heritage in mind, the traditional and convoluted features are given a modern twist. A big chandelier hangs from the ceiling while light floods the dining room through long windows. Mint-green walls provide a royal atmosphere. Chef and restaurant owner Cyril Lignac has dedicated his cuisine to fresh fish and focuses on traditional French cooking techniques and modernised versions.

1 Rue Jules Vallès, 75011 Paris
www.restaurantlechardenoux.com

DRINK

LA COMMUNE

VIBRANT AND CLASSY

With hip hop blasting from the speaker, waxed concrete walls, corrugated plastic, green marble countertops and brass seats, La Commune is vibrant and classy and ready to serve the house specialty: punches to share. Cocktails are concocted with selected ingredients and French alcohol (particularly Rhum) is served in silver bowls, for example, the homemade Falernum Syrup Planter, lemon, fennel, mint, cucumber with a tad of sparkling water. All sorts of gently spiced cocktails are made, sometimes with French whiskey. To snack? Different and very nice tapas (hummus, paté, cheese/ham plate, hot dog etc.) are available!

80 Boulevard de Belleville, 75020 Paris
www.syndicatcocktailclub.com

SERPENT À PLUME

PARIS' BEST-KEPT SECRET

Cafe, cocktails and pyjamas. Serpent à Plume is a concept that flirts with the irrational. Discreetly hidden under the arcades of the Place des Vosges, it is without doubt, Paris' best-kept secret. Nightlife at Serpent à Plume has nothing to do with nightclubs or spending money, yet it is complete nightlife in the truest sense. Typical evenings are spent among characters worlds away from reality. The cocktail bar with its 70s retro-chic design mixed with pre-Colombian art and old American rock soundtrack reminds one of the Grand Budapest Hotel and the drinks are considered ultra-gourmet cocktails, made to be sipped in the jacuzzi.

24 Place des Vosges, 75003 Paris
www. serpentaplume.com

GRAVITY BAR

FASHIONABLE COCKTAIL BAR

Gravity is the programme at this cocktail bar. It lures Paris' trendy clientele like a magnet and makes the Rue des Vinaigriers one of the city's hottest streets. This is thanks in part to its self-consciously stylish interior – the ceiling is covered with vertical wave-shaped slats that seem to crash down dramatically behind the massive steel counter. Less overtly ambitious, but equally striking, is the charming little terrace outside with its sleek, Scandinavian-style furnishings. Gravity Bar offers wild concoctions that are vibrant and well balanced. Here, size does matter as the drinks are generous. A particular delight is the Fruit du Passé, made from Strega liquor, Genepi Dolin, homemade celery syrup, lemon juice, liquorice powder and fennel seeds.

44 Rue des Vinaigriers, 75010 Paris

FITZGERALD

EXQUISITE LONG DRINKS

One bar one motto: give an experience to the customers. The Fitzgerald in the 7th arrondissement attracts trendy 30-year-olds like a magnet. This place is more sophisticated than anything in Paris. Talented mixologists concoct wild and unique cocktails in an interior reminiscent of the Roaring Twenties. The barkeeper boss is a bubbly Italian woman who makes exquisite Long Drinks.

Just order a Ruby Waterfall, an El Salvador, or a Croissant de Lune and let the magic work. For a special event, groups or couples can go into the séparée, a secret salon with glam velvet banquettes, 50s pink flamingo wallpaper, copper details and lowered lights to flirt quietly.

54 Boulevard de la Tour-Maubourg, 75007 Paris
www.fitzgerald.paris

DÉV!ANT

DÉVIANT

POPULAR AMONG CREATIVES

Déviant is a stand-up restaurant inspired by the Savoir Vivre's president Arnaud Lacombe and Vivant's chef Pierre Touitou. Two executive chefs work on new recipes every day to keep the dishes innovative. This buzzy, marble- and terrazzo-clad natural-wine bar in the lively 10th arrondissement also celebrates generations-old traditional family recipes. Déviant has slightly tweaked the recipes to make them more crowd-friendly. Popular among creatives, the restaurant seems to be a never-ending block party. Its original sister restaurant, Vivant, a 19-seater neo-bistro, is located just four doors down.

39 Rue des Petites Écuries, 75010 Paris
www.vivantparis.com

ISTR

FLESHY OYSTERS & DELIGHTFUL DRINKS

Istr is a bar-restaurant located in Rue Notre-Dame de Nazareth in Paris' 3rd arrondissement. On the menu are fleshy oysters, delightful cocktails, small and original dishes and natural wines. These can be enjoyed at the counter, or in a corner of the room papered with patterned wallpaper depicting big crabs and turnips. Inspired by a New York oyster bar, Istr is chic yet unfussy. Istr offers useful additions such as USB sockets to charge a phone under the bar. In addition to the oysters and punchy appetisers, Istr also offers tapas: pollock ceviche, salmon gravlax or cauliflower tabbouleh.

41 Rue Notre Dame de Nazareth, 75003 Paris

istr

60

DANICO

BROOKLYN-STYLE BAR

Danico is the bar attached to hotspot Daroco, a large light, and chic Italian eatery, all housed in Jean Paul Gaultier's former flagship. The bar, located in Paris' oldest gallery, Galerie Vivienne, is a trendy Brooklyn-style bar complete with high ceilings, green velvet armchairs, black and white striped marble bar and good soundtracks.

The masterminds behind it are Nico de Soto, Thibault Mequignon and his team. Their approach to drinks is inspired by travels and cuisine, always trying to get new flavours, combinations and techniques. Today Danico is ranked 73rd in the World's 100 Best Bars.

6 Rue Vivienne, 75002 Paris

MOLITOR

ROOFTOP BAR MOLITOR

A MYTHICAL PLACE SINCE THE 30S

Molitor is an institution in the "City of Lights", first opened in 1929. Then it was the most popular swimming bath venue, known for its two swimming pools and avant-garde atmosphere. Today, Molitor is much more than just a swimming pool. It is a hotel with 124 rooms and suites, and also a restaurant open to everyone, proposing fresh summer dishes for the Rooftop with meze, plancha and grills by Lebanese chef Nader Hassan and his crew. And, Molitor is a club offering an alternative to the city rush. Till today, it is an audacious, constantly evolving location for those who want to experience the unusual.

13 Rue Nungesser et Coli, 75016 Paris
www.mltr.fr

SHOP

THE SOCIALITE FAMILY

LIFESTYLE AND INTERIOR DESIGN

This shop offers home design and the lifestyle for contemporary families. Whether in Paris, London, New York or Milan, these families all share their unique vision on how to harmonise family life and interior design. At 12 Rue Saint-Fiacre in Paris' 2nd arrondissement, the whole universe comes alive in a stylish and welcoming setting of Milanese influence, punctuated by references to the childhood of founder and artistic director Constance Gennari. The entrance halls are typical 1960s, they remind the owner of her upbringing. Mahogany wood on the walls adds warmth, punctuated here and there by subtle touches of brass. The main colours here are terracotta, mustard or green, which were selected by Constance for the boutique as it recalls her Italy and fits very well with the travertine, brass and wood.

12 Rue Saint-Fiacre, 75002 Paris
www.thesocialitefamily.com

NOSE

BEAUTY CONCEPT STORE

Welcome to the most beautiful nose of Paris. The Nose beauty store is situated in the 2nd arrondissement in the Rue Bachaumont, between bakeries, restaurants and fashion labels. The shop carries hundreds of scents from all over the world and is a Mecca for all perfume lovers. The primary focus is to establish an olfactory diagnostic to find one's own ideal fragrance. Within 30 minutes, one will have received up to 10 personalised recommendations from over 700 designer fragrances. Besides perfume, Nose has a carefully curated selection of beauty products and scented candles, which can be purchased from the online shop as well. Nose is at the forefront of the French perfume industry.

20 Rue Bachaumont, 75002 Paris
www.noseparis.com

202

À REBOURS

CONTEMPORARY OBJECTS

À Rebours is a small novelty shop fuelled by the big ambitions of creation. Located in the Marais district, this concept store is a multidisciplinary production and exhibition space for contemporary artists, designers and creative producers of every facet. With the "À Rebours", have developed a salesroom for the assortment of products. The store offers contemporary objects – very few of which are available elsewhere. Unusual, witty, useful and quirky, the selection is an answer to the emergence of new forms of production and consumption. À Rebours is the outpost for a conscious trade, open to the ideas that transform and embellish our daily life.

46 Rue Sainte-Croix de la Bretonnerie, 75004 Paris

ARCHIVE 18-20

CONCEPT STORE FOR MEN

Archive 18-20 is a label, a unique store space in Paris, offering experiences, fashion and lifestyle curation, art gallery and coffee. Behind the gate of an old Parisian building hides a parenthesis. Under the immense luminous glass roof unfolds an area of $450m^2$, where time is suspended. In this urban garden of a new kind, fashion is the reflection of a lifestyle in which Severine Lahyani the founder, offers a selection of rare objects and pieces by established or emerging creators, vintage pieces, plant installations; editing each of her choices to offer a personal vision of contemporary creation.

20 Rue des Archives, 75004 Paris
www.archive1820.com

EMPREINTES

THE FRENCH CRAFT CONCEPT STORE

Empreintes Paris is the concept store for French craftsmanship. Craftsmen from all around France display their work in this magnificent 600sqm at the heart of the iconic Marais district in Rue de Picardie. The Picasso Museum is also located here. Over 1 000 different objects that include furniture, accessories, tableware, decorations, sculptures and jewellery are spread over four floors and lit up by large windows. Handmade in France, all the objects on display are either one-of-a-kind or limited-edition pieces that would otherwise be impossible to find. Empreintes supports and organises the work of over 6 000 craftsmen, artists and independent manufacturers.

5 Rue de Picardie, 75003 Paris
www.empreintes-paris.com

MAISON SARAH LAVOINE

DESIGN FURNITURE STUDIO

At Maison Sarah Lavoine one finds wonderful variations of highlighted original pieces, furniture with noble materials that vibrate emotion and a desire for infinity. This design studio dares to blend blues to create harmony in daily life and offers everything from interior design to paint collections, lightings to linen, cushions to clothing, and furniture and objects to curated products. Over 100 retail partners sell Lavoine's interior-design signature across the globe. It incorporates a mix of styles and origins, elegance and comfort, the embodiment of a cosmopolitan Parisian spirit. Maison Sarah Lavoine is a definition of the art of living, accessible luxury and most of all, an optimistic view of life.

6 Place des Victoires, 75002 Paris
www. sarahlavoine.com

L'ESTHETIQUE
DU
DEPLAISIR

YVON LAMBERT GALLERY

ART GALLERY AND BOOKSHOP

Yvon Lambert is a contemporary art gallery and bookshop founded by Yvon Lambert in 1966. Lambert is a key figure in the art world who promotes the works of the most innovating artists. Yvon Lambert's bookshop specialises in art books, limited edition works, exhibition catalogues, artist's books and rare and out of print books. Yvon Lambert is known as the famous 83-year-old contemporary art gallerist in France. Located in the historic Marais district on the Rue des Filles du Calvaire, art lovers often find a spot to sit and read under the Parisian sun after buying an art book.

14 Rue des Filles du Calvaire, 75003 Paris
shop.yvon-lambert.com

MERCI

FASHION & HOME STORE

Tucked away in a backyard on the Boulevard Beaumarchais is the entrance to a concept store named "Merci". This is also its motto: proceeds from sales are donated in part to aid projects, especially in Madagascar.
From fashion items, furniture, bedding, books, and art supplies to designer ornaments, kitchen accessories and jewellery, pretty much everything is sold in this attractive 1,500sqm location. Bright light shines on the wooden panels and invites guests to browse and relax and perhaps find a treasure.

111 Boulevard Beaumarchais, 75003 Paris
www.merci-merci.com

THE BROKEN ARM

COFFEE AND CLOTHING

Hiding on a street corner in the middle of the Marais district, The Broken Arm offers coffee and clothing. This boutique concept store has no more than 20 seats, just enough to enjoy coffee and cake and watch people go by. Breakfast offerings include avocado toast and granola, while lunch includes tasty delights like soups, salads and sourdough bread. Selling all kinds of men's and women's clothing items, The Broken Arm Paris was founded in 2013 by entrepreneurs Guillaume Steinmetz, Anaïs Lafarge and Romain Joste. Before venturing into the real-life retail space, this team ran the lifestyle and fashion website De Jeunes Gens Modernes.

12 Rue Perrée, 75003 Paris
www.the-broken-arm.com

LA GARÇONNIERE

DEDICATED TO MEN'S LIFESTYLE

This project is an initiative of four young brands: Oncle Pape, Apto, Newstalk and Monsieur London. This store, located in the Marais district, personifies Parisian lifestyle and fulfils the dreams of fashionistas. Why? A bold selection of the latest trends and a casual welcome can be found here. In short, La Garçonnière represents the vision of the trade, where "buy" should be just one word among many others: discover, taste, play, relax, share and laugh. All the products are displayed on shelves leaning against raw brick walls. Leafy greens and a white floor brighten up the space and invite every visitor to enter and explore.

47 Rue des Archives, 75003 Paris
www.la-garconniere.fr

ASTIER DE VILLATTE SAINT-HONORÉ

MAGICAL & TWIRLY CERAMICS

Located in the Rue Saint-Honoré, Astier de Vilatte offers magical and twirly ceramics and other products, such as masks, floral balls, joke articles and Moleskine magazines from Italy, Japan and America. Two friends, designer Ivan Pericoli and Benoît Astier de Villatte had the idea to create a shop dedicated to ceramics and other curious creations. The pottery is made in the company's studio on Boulevard Masséna, exhibited and sold in its boutique in the originally restored rooms from 1778. The numerous Parisian second-hand stores and flea markets are a source of great inspiration for the various products.

173 Rue Saint-Honoré, 75001 Paris
www.astierdevillatte.com

EXPLORE

At the gates of Paris stretches the world's largest flea market - home to 14 individual markets and more than 1,500 stall holders. From antique jewellery and furniture to vintage clothes, Saint-Ouen, is the perfect address for vintage lovers and fashionistas. In the explore category you'll find personally selected stores and restaurants at this vibrant Parisian flea market.

MAISON JAUNE DESIGN

RARE PIECES, MATERIALS AND LIGHTS

Maison Jaune enables people to see, breathe and appreciate art. This interior design gallery offers a subtle mix of rare pieces, materials and lights. It is an expression of the philosophy of Elodie and Julien who define their studio as an eclectic, unexpected and convivial meeting between the past and the present. Maison Jaune is a vintage store that provides a service for customers around interior design, decoration and scenography.

96 Rue des Rosiers, Stand 145 Allée 3, 93400 Saint-Ouen
www.maisonjaunedesign.com

MA COCOTTE

MODERN YET COZY RESTAURANT

Ma Cocotte is the iconic restaurant in the flea market of Saint-Ouen. It is part of the group of bistros owned by Hakim Gaouaoui and Norbert Tarayre, a famous chef featured on French TV. Ma Cocotte offers gourmet and homemade bistro cuisine at low prices. The pleasant terraces are divine in Parisian sunny weather, while the interior, designed by Philippe Starck, is beauty for the eyes. The menu is renewed every four weeks.

106 Rue des Rosiers, 93400 Saint-Ouen
www.macocotte-lespuces.com

TALKING HEADS
Franz Ferdinand
GITANES
Fumer tue

AURÉLIEN JEAUNEAU

SERIOUS ANTIQUE DEALER

Buying French design from the second half of the 20th century is no problem with Aurélien Jeauneau. The young antique dealer strives and regularly offers signed and referenced pieces from Pierre Guariche, Pierre Paulin, Joseph-Andre Motte, Robert Debièvre, Michel Mortier, Louis Paolozzi, Geneviève Dangles and Christian de France, among others. Passionate about his profession and his specialisation, Aurélien Jeauneau is recognised as a serious antique dealer. Located at the Paul Bert market in Saint-Ouen, he also hosts exhibitions. Why shop online, if one can rediscover the pleasure of hunting, adventure and learning about beautiful designer objects. Aurélien Jeauneau adds an original touch, that's rich in aesthetics and history, too.

Marché Paul Bert, Alley6 Booth93, Saint-Ouen

MARKOTTE CAFE

ZERO-WASTE CAFE

This restaurant is indeed innovative: to make organic food accessible to everyone, Markotte tackles food waste by recovering unsold products at a lower cost. Located close to the famous flea markets of Saint-Ouen, the very essence of Markotte's DNA is cooking good organic dishes using the foods in their entirety. Nothing is thrown away. Everything is cooked. Zero stock, zero remains and zero waste. The concept was developed by Chloé Charles, a young rising star of French cuisine specialising in anti-waste. Whether indulging in breakfast or afternoon tea, craft beers and organic wines, each guest leaves with a hand-made scrub pot made by Markotte's team, from the coffee grounds of the day.

21 rue du Plaisir, 93400 Saint-Ouen
www. markotte.com

MOB HOTEL

ETHICAL & CULTURAL EMBASSY

MOB offers a modern, healthy and peaceful space, where everyone is invited to enjoy a unique place where action and events combine to raise awareness among people to respect the environment, including among others: an almost zero use of plastic; the sorting of waste; and partnerships with international associations like Good Planet. A huge orange door decorated with a protection symbol invites each guest inside. At the MOB Hotel, visitors relax in unpretentious designer rooms. The entire interior is comfortable and effortlessly stylish. Guests can relax while eating in the organic restaurant and enjoying summertime garden buzzes, not to mention the last minute musical surprises and the outdoor cinema. The largest flea market in Europe is only a few minutes walk away and adds to the dream of lounging in style in Paris. More than a hotel, MOB is a place of life both festive and zen.

6 Rue Gambetta, 93400 Saint-Ouen
www.mobhotel.com/paris